I0139463

Healing After a Suicide Loss

All Ages Workbook + Activity Guide

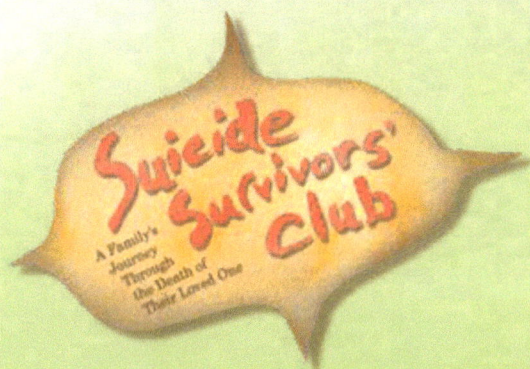

Suicide Survivors' Club

A Family's Journey Through the Death of Their Loved One

Laurie Phillips

Rebecca Anderson

ADVISORS
Noel Larson, PhD, MSW
Janice Nadeau, PhD, LP, RN, Bereavement Specialist
Jenny Simmonds, MEd, Fairview Youth Grief Services
Sue Towey, APRN, CNS, MS, Integrative Mental Health Practitioner

"The SSC workbook, along with the beautiful book set, invites you into the creative wisdom of an authentic personal path of healing. The Anderson family has courageously shared their individual stories using an organic healing process of storytelling and art. The workbook is a guide that offers the reader a way to find their own authentic voice of healing from the trauma of suicide."

Sue Towey, APRN, MS, (retired LP), Integrative Mental Health

"I recommend this book for those bereaved by a suicide death, and for any professionals who strive to give well-informed, compassionate care to suicide survivors of any age."

Janice Winchester Nadeau, PhD, LP, RN, Bereavement Specialist

"These books provide an integrated approach for healing and speak to what I call a revolution in the mental health world, a revolution that we all hope will save lives."

Noel R. Larson, Ph.D., Clinical Psychologist

"Healing After a Suicide Loss: All Ages Workbook + Activity Guide offers hands-on guidance borne out of personal experience and ongoing research. The perspective is unique, showing that it is not only possible to survive a loved one's suicide, but also to find meaning and learn to thrive again after such a difficult loss. The combination of authentic experience, meaningfully supportive stories, and creative activities help access the healing power for suicide survivors. I am proud to wholeheartedly endorse this guide."

Henry Emmons, MD, author of The Chemistry of Calm and The Chemistry of Joy and creator of the Joy Lab podcast

Healing After a Suicide Loss

All Ages Workbook + Activity Guide

Laurie Phillips

Rebecca Anderson

ADVISORS
Noel Larson, PhD, MSW
Janice Nadeau, PhD, LP, RN, Bereavement Specialist
Jenny Simmonds, MEd, Fairview Youth Grief Services
Sue Towey, APRN, CNS, MS, Integrative Mental Health Practitioner

RESOURCE *Publications* · Eugene, Oregon

Healing After a Suicide Loss
All Ages Workbook + Activity Guide

Resource Publications
An Imprint of Wipf and Stock Publishers
199 W. 8th Ave., Suite 3
Eugene, OR 97401

www.wipfandstock.com

PAPERBACK ISBN: 979-8-3852-5091-2
HARDCOVER ISBN: 979-8-3852-5092-9
EBOOK ISBN: 979-8-3852-5093-6

This book is dedicated to suicide loss survivors of all ages.

CONTRIBUTORS
SSC Team: Laurie Phillips, Rebecca Anderson, Louise Woehrle, Aidan Anderson

Mental Health Advisors: Noel Larson, PhD, MSW; Janice Nadeau, PhD, LP, RN, Bereavement Specialist; Jenny Simmonds, MEd, Fairview Youth Grief Services; Sue Towey, APRN, CNS, MS, Integrative Mental Health Practitioner

Artist Advisors: Maarja Roth, Susan Gangsei

Suicide Survivors' Club LLC does not offer counseling.
The information provided here is to be used for supportive purposes only and is not intended to replace the advice of any professional who may be caring for or assisting you.

Story Portrait™ is trademarked by Laurie Phillips.

The activity pages in this book may be reproduced, copied, and distributed for non-commercial purposes by therapists and facilitators for use with their clients and groups.

Ordering information: www.SuicideSurvivorsClub.org

Introduction

Not knowing what was ahead for us — or how to get there — required me, the kids, and our friends to wear many hats. We wore miner's helmets when we were trying to excavate the truth of what had happened to Don and to us. We were explorers in pith helmets as we entered the emotional jungle of PTSD and mourning, simply doing our best to put one foot in front of the other. All of our journeys as a family resulted in discoveries, stories and knowledge.

Excerpt from Parenting the Suicide Survivors' Club

To Suicide Loss Survivors

You're reading this book because you've lost someone to suicide. Maybe it was your spouse, your parent, your child, or a sister or brother. Maybe it was your friend.

I lost my husband, Don, to suicide in 2002. It was a shattering experience for me and our children, who were 5, 7, and 19 years old. Our story about how we each experienced Don's death and how we healed afterwards is described in the books, *Suicide Survivors' Club: A Family's Journey Through the Death of Their Loved One,* a collaboration with artist Laurie Phillips.

What Laurie and I want you to know is that even though it may not seem possible right now, you can eventually recover your life and even feel joy again. We created this workbook and activity guide to help you move in that direction.

You'll find questions based on shared experiences of loss that you can write about. You'll also find activities meant to open up new ways of looking at what you're going through and put it into a different context.

You're not alone on your journey. My children and I have gone through it and received help. You can too.

To Therapists, Educators, and Facilitators

This workbook is meant as a tool to assist you as you help clients, students, or groups who have lost someone to suicide. Thank you for the immensely important, compassionate work you do.

–Rebecca Anderson

For Suicide Loss Survivors

You'll find questions and activities created for three age groups — kids (age 6-11), teens (age 12-18), and adults (age 19+). Each age group has the same five themes: *How Did You Find Out, Life Now, What's Helpful and What's Not, Feelings*, and *Remembering Your Special Person*.

Find the section you want to use by looking for the color-coded tabs.

Kids Age 6-11..........page 6-17

Teens Age 12-18..........page 18-29

Adults Age 19+..........page 30-41

There are pages from the *Suicide Survivors' Club* books in the workbook that show an example of how each member of the Anderson family experienced various feelings and reactions after the death of their husband/father. Their examples might help you write about your life.

Reflecting about yourself through writing and doing activities can show you a different perspective that validates your experience. Loss can make you feel isolated and alone, but self-reflection with compassion can knit you back into the fabric of human life.

Adults might find it helpful to do the activities meant for kids, and teens might prefer writing on the adult questions. Feel free to experiment.

You can come back to these questions and activities in a week, a month, a year — and see how you've changed.

Note: Throughout this book you'll see blank lines you can fill in with the name of the person who died — Dad, Mom, Uncle Bill, Susie, Mark — so you can refer to them in a way that feels right for you.

For Therapists, Educators, and Facilitators

Individual Activities Page 6-41

If you're working one-on-one with a client you might introduce the journaling questions and individual activities by saying, "We'll use the stories told by Will, Aidan, Pattie, and Becky as a way to help you with your loss. Choose one you most relate to and we'll start there."

You might photocopy activities like the measuring cup on page 7 or the doodling on page 18 and use them for every client visit as a check for how they're feeling that day.

Note: Throughout this book there are blank lines the survivor can fill in with the name of their loved one — Dad, Mom, Uncle Bill, Susie, Mark — so they can be referred to in a way that feels right for the survivor.

Group Activities Page 42-47

If you're leading a group for children, teens or adults, you'll find three activities you can use. Objectives for the activities are:

- Share openly in a safe, creative environment
- Encourage and recognize the expression of feelings through engaging and creative means
- Establish that they're are not to blame for the suicide
- Acknowledge the complex feelings arising from their loss

Helpful Resources

Page 48-51

A GUIDE FOR FRIENDS: WHAT TO SAY… AND WHAT NOT TO SAY Six tips based on what loss survivors say they need and want.

SAFE MESSAGING How to talk about suicide in your communities and on social media.

HELPFUL ORGANIZATIONS A list of crisis hotlines, text lines, and information about suicide and mental illness.

WARNING SIGNS OF SUICIDE What to do if your family member, friend, or acquaintance displays these signs.

Kids

heaven

I'm 5 years old. We're upstairs in the living room when my Mom tells us my Dad died. My sister is there too, we're all crying.

hell

1. Will describes being in the living room with his Mom, his sister and his brother when he was told that his Dad had died. Everyone was crying.

- How did you find out _____ had died?
- Where were you?
- Who else was there?
- What did you do?

_____

_____

_____

_____

ACTIVITY

Color in the amount on each measuring cup to show how you felt when you found out _____ had died.

How **confused** did you feel when you first heard?

A LOT
— 3/4 —
— 1/2 —
— 1/4 —
A LITTLE

How **scared** did you feel when you first heard?

A LOT
— 3/4 —
— 1/2 —
— 1/4 —
A LITTLE

How **loved** did you feel when you first heard?

A LOT
— 3/4 —
— 1/2 —
— 1/4 —
A LITTLE

2. Will remembered going to school the same day he found out his Dad died. But his Mom says he didn't go back to school for over a week. Grief can sometimes confuse our memories.

- What was it like when you returned to school?
- How did your friends learn about the death?

I go to school later that day and the teacher announces to everyone that my Dad has died.

ACTIVITY

Make stick figure drawings for each box.

Draw the person who helped
you feel okay when went back
to school

Draw what you ate for lunch when you
went back to school

Draw what you did during a break time
when you went back to school

Draw what helped you feel safe
when you went back to school

What do you notice about your drawings? _____

_____

_____

_____

The next week we start therapy. We talk about feelings and play with toys. I love the fake burgers, old board games and costumes. Mom wears a tiara, I wear a policeman's hat and whistle.

3. Will was helped by using costumes and games to express how he felt.

- What Halloween costume or favorite character shows how you feel right now?

- What could that character say to the rest of the world to explain what you're going through?

- What could they say to you that would be helpful?

ACTIVITY

Fill the talk bubbles with words that describe:
- Things people said that hurt your feelings
- Things people said that helped you feel better

4. Will was helped by talking to a therapist about his feelings. You probably have lots of feelings too. How do you like to express them?

- Do you have friends you talk to?
- What toys or games do you play with?
- Do you like to draw?
- Do you play music or sports?

We go to Dad's grave and put flowers on it every year.

After awhile we stop going to therapy except for checkins.

ACTIVITY

Put a check mark on the statements that feel true for you right now. All these feelings are okay!

My friendships are different now.

It's harder for me to concentrate at school.

My role and responsibilities in my family have changed.

There is less fighting at home.

I get angry a lot — even over little things.

People treat me differently.

I feel afraid most of the time.

I don't feel anything about what happened.

Sometimes I feel like it was my fault.

I feel more peaceful.

My home feels really different.

I have a lot of questions about suicide and wonder why they killed themselves.

I worry about who else might die.

It's harder for me to talk about suicide.

My parent cries a lot more.

I can't stop thinking about it.

I feel invisible, like people don't see me.

It's easier for me to talk about suicide.

5. Will saw that he loved astronomy and engineering just like his Dad.

• What things are you interested in that _____ was interested in too? (Cooking, sports, reading, fishing, knitting, gardening, drawing, music, video games, traveling, and movies, for example.)

• What things are you interested in that they were not interested in?

_____

_____

_____

_____

_____

_____

_____

_____

_____

_____

_____

I really like science—astronomy and engineering. I definitely inherited that from my Dad. He was gone so I've just explored it on my own.

ACTIVITY

Draw a picture of your special person's favorite foods.

– Which of these foods do you like too?

– Which ones would you never eat?

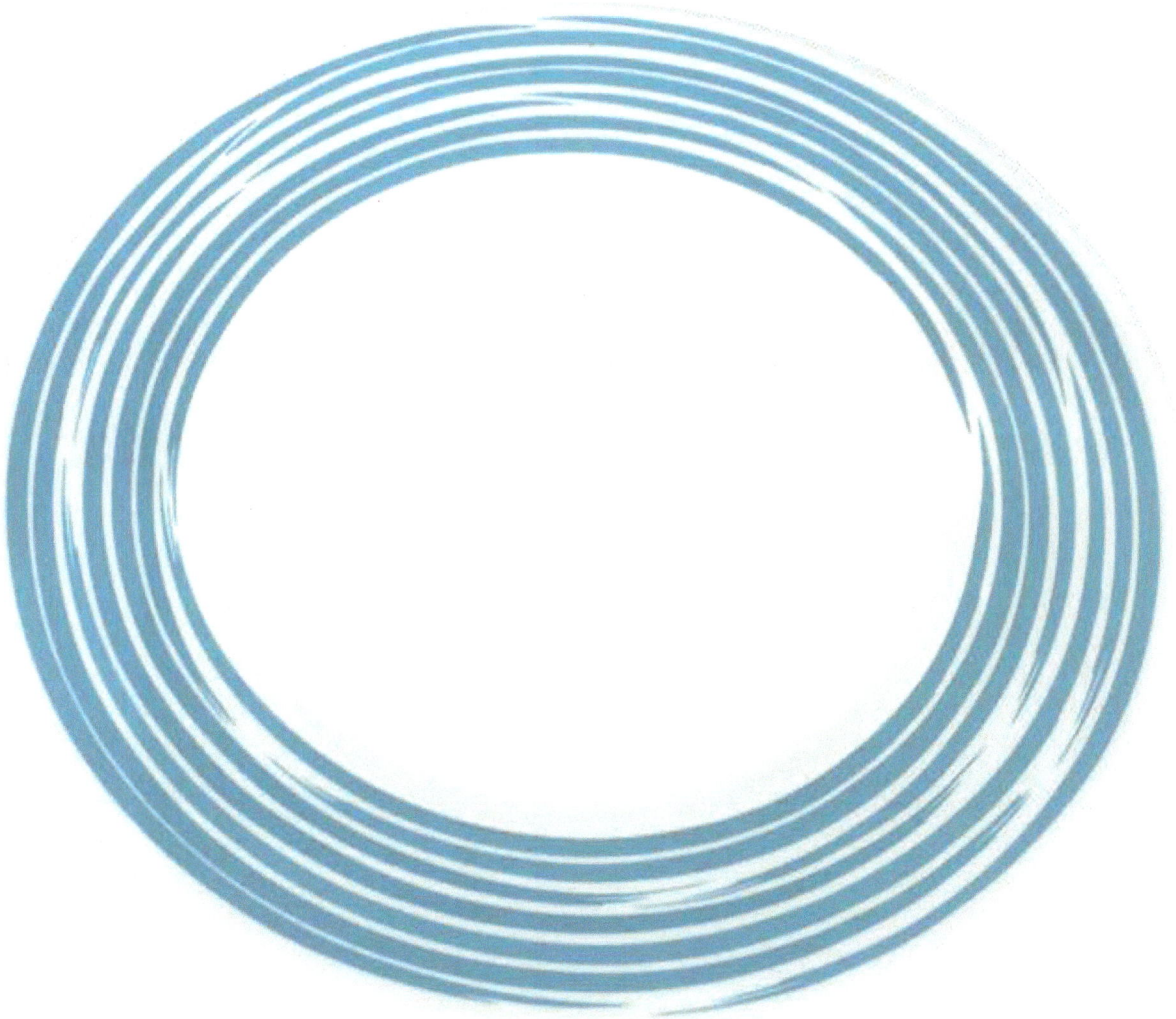

BONUS ACTIVITY

Write, doodle, or draw your answers to the following questions.

What do you wish you had said to _____ before they died?

What do you regret saying to _____ before they died?

If you could somehow get a message to _____ right now, what would you say?

Write a goodbye letter to _____, sharing your thoughts and your feelings.

Teens

ACTIVITY

Doodle for five minutes. Try to fill up the page below with scribbling or a pattern that expresses how you feel right now about the loss of _____.

I GET HOME AND TWO FAMILY FRIENDS ARE THERE. MY MOM TAKES ME UPSTAIRS AND TELLS ME THAT MY DAD IS DEAD. HE WAS FOUND IN A PARK AFTER KILLING HIMSELF.

1. Pattie found out what happened from her Mom.

- How did you find out?
- If someone told you, what words did they use?
- Who else was there?
- Did you have a physical reaction, like in your chest or stomach? Or did you feel numb?

_____

_____

_____

_____

_____

_____

_____

_____

_____

2. Pattie's first thought after she found out her dad died was about who would walk her down the aisle when she got married.

• What was your first thought about how your life would be different?

MY FIRST THOUGHT IS "OH MY GOD, WHO WILL WALK ME DOWN THE AISLE?" EVEN THOUGH I'M NOT EVEN IN A RELATIONSHIP.

ACTIVITY

Close your eyes and let your finger land on an activity that will help you feel calm and present. Do that activity for one minute.

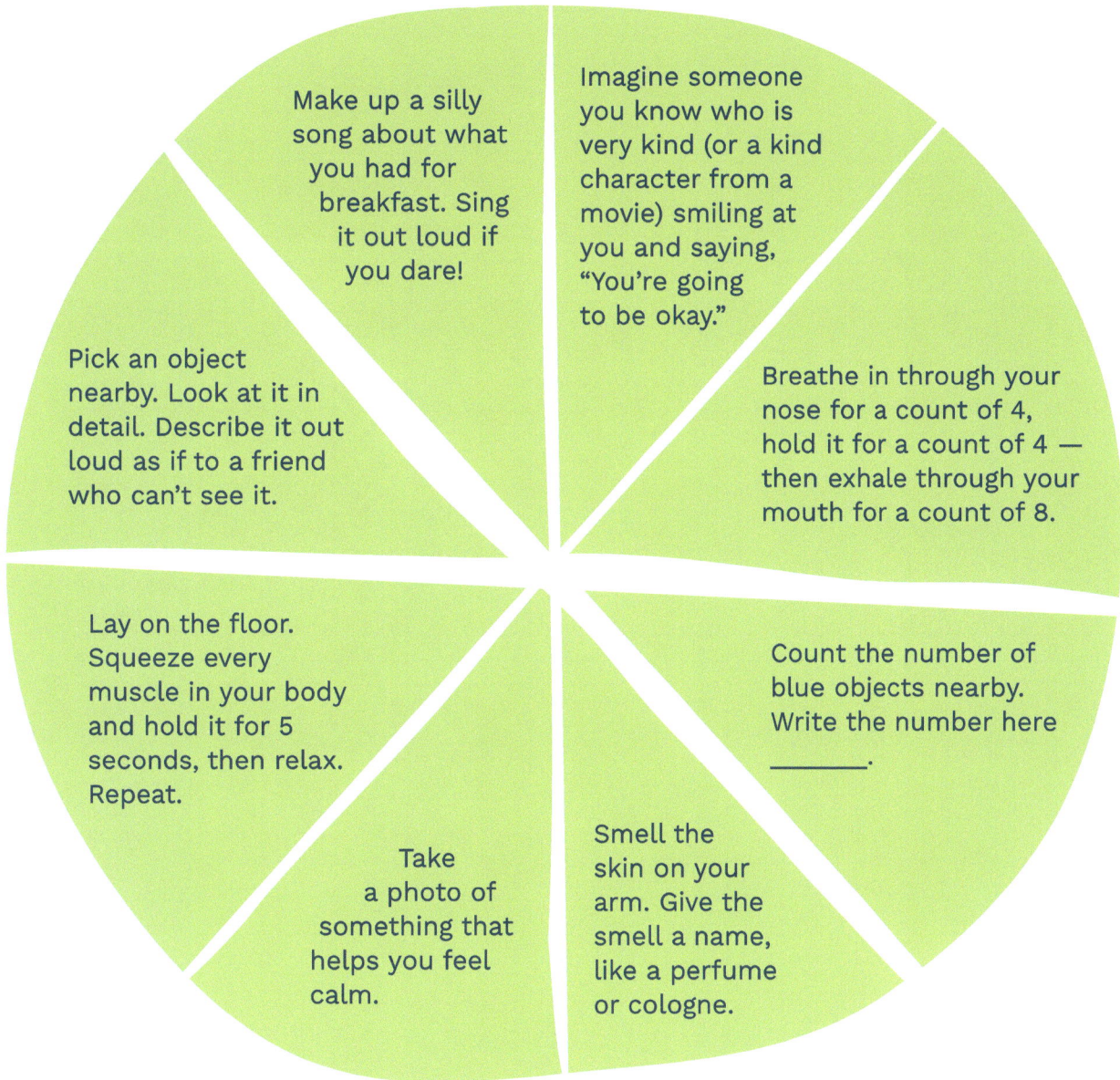

Make up a silly song about what you had for breakfast. Sing it out loud if you dare!

Imagine someone you know who is very kind (or a kind character from a movie) smiling at you and saying, "You're going to be okay."

Pick an object nearby. Look at it in detail. Describe it out loud as if to a friend who can't see it.

Breathe in through your nose for a count of 4, hold it for a count of 4 — then exhale through your mouth for a count of 8.

Lay on the floor. Squeeze every muscle in your body and hold it for 5 seconds, then relax. Repeat.

Count the number of blue objects nearby. Write the number here _____.

Take a photo of something that helps you feel calm.

Smell the skin on your arm. Give the smell a name, like a perfume or cologne.

3. Aidan's principal, teacher, and fellow students gave him gifts.

- How did your friends, classmates, and teachers treat you when you returned to school?
- What did your classmates say to you?
- What did you say to your classmates?
- How did you feel?

_____

_____

_____

When I come back everyone asks what happened. A few parents tell their kids that my Dad died in a car crash. Some kids think I was out sick. I tell them the truth.

I miss 2 weeks of school. The principal, my 2nd grade teacher and students give me a basket full of toys.

I have to make up all the schoolwork I missed.

_____

_____

_____

_____

_____

_____

ACTIVITY

Put a check mark by the emojis that reflect how you felt about going back to school and reconnecting with friends and teachers.

Draw your own emojis that describe your experience.

It's honestly hard to imagine life with my Dad now, we've gone for so long without him.

I feel sad and furious with my father and get some therapy for my feelings.

4. Aidan got used to life without his dad, but he still had feelings of sadness and anger that he went to a therapist for help with.

- Who have you felt safe enough to talk to — a family member, a friend, a teacher, a therapist, someone from your place of worship?

- Do you think of _____ as having a mental illness?

- Do you think their mental illness contributed to their suicide?

ACTIVITY

It's normal to feel a mixture of emotions that change frequently. Circle the rock that describes how you feel right now in each area.

ANGRY ——————————————————————————— ACCEPTING

FRUSTRATED ——————————————————————————— CALM

HOPELESS ——————————————————————————— HOPEFUL

ALONE ——————————————————————————— CONNECTED

SCARED ——————————————————————————— BRAVE

If you shared this page with someone, who would you choose?

_____.

ACTIVITY

1. What memories of _____ do you want to keep? Go for a walk or find small objects in your house that represent these memories (a rock, a coin, a pen, a note in their handwriting).

2. What memories do you want to put away for now? Find different objects that represent these memories.

3. Find a box (maybe a shoe box). Place the memories you want to put away on the bottom of the box and cover them with paper or cloth.

4. Place the "keeper" memory objects on top where you can see them.

5. Find a special place for your box.

I KNOW THAT NO MATTER HOW BAD IT GETS, THINGS ALWAYS GET BETTER. I STILL HAVE TROUBLE TALKING ABOUT MY DAD'S SUICIDE — I DON'T WANT PEOPLE PITYING ME OR THINKING I'M DIFFERENT. IT TAKES ME AWHILE TO TELL MY NEW BOYFRIEND, BUT WHEN I DO, HE'S GREAT ABOUT IT.

I'M LIVING IN A BEAUTIFUL PLACE BY THE WATER WHERE I CAN SEE THE STARS AT NIGHT. MY DAD USED TO TELL ME STORIES ABOUT THE CONSTELLATIONS. HE LOVED THE WATER TOO.

5. Pattie thought about her dad when she saw the stars at night because he used to tell her about the constellations. He loved the water, and that also reminded Pattie of her dad.

• What places keep _____ alive in your heart?

• Is there something like an animal, a car, a song, the stars, etc., that reminds you of them?

BONUS ACTIVITY

Write, doodle, or draw your answers to the following questions.

What do you wish you had said to _____ before they died?

What do you regret saying to _____ before they died?

If you could somehow get a message to _____ right now, what would you say?

Write a goodbye letter to _____, sharing your thoughts and your feelings.

Adults

Don takes the kids to school. I call several times to ask him to meet me for lunch so we can talk. He refuses. I know something is wrong.

He doesn't show up to meet me and the kids for their swimming lesson. I call Pattie and ask if he called her. She says no. I don't want to call 911 so I ask a family friend to see if her father, the local fire chief, can send a police car to the park where I believe Don is.

Two squad cars pull up and come to the door and ask my name. They tell me Don has killed himself.

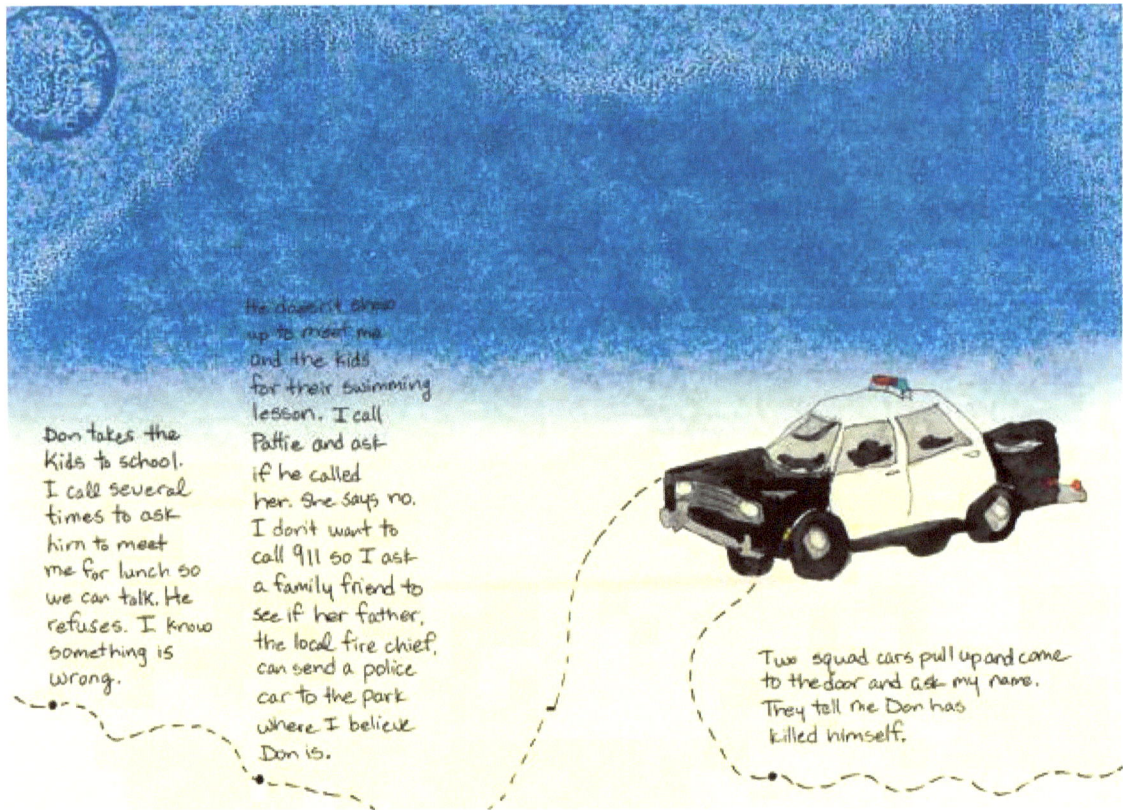

1. On the day that Don died, Becky knew something was wrong because he didn't want to meet her for lunch, he didn't show up for the kids' swimming lesson and then he didn't answer the phone.

- On the day _____ died, what was the first sign that something was wrong?

- How did you discover what happened?

- What was your immediate reaction after you heard what happened?

- What was your experience with the police or medical professionals like?

- What did you need soon after you heard what happened?

_____

_____

_____

_____

_____

_____

_____

_____

_____

_____

_____

_____

_____

_____

ACTIVITY

You're going to be okay

Write yourself an encouraging message using a post-it note, greeting card, email, text, or voicemail.

Find a quiet time to let your heart take in the words.

Put it in a place you'll see it often.

2. After the memorial service Becky had to return to daily life and post-traumatic stress set in.

•   What was it like for you to return to daily life?

•   What were some of the unpleasant tasks you had to take on?

•   Were you able to ask for help?

•   If others made suggestions about how to take care of yourself, which ones were the most helpful?

•   What things in your life are easier or better without _____?

_____

_____

_____

_____

_____

_____

_____

_____

_____

The legal paperwork is endless: banks, lawyers, social security, taxes, wills.

We celebrate Halloween, Thanksgiving and Christmas. It's bleak and painful.

ACTIVITY

Close your eyes and let your finger land on an activity that will help you feel calm and present.

Make up a silly song using the words you just wrote on the previous page. Sing it out loud if you can.

Imagine someone you know who's very kind (or a kind character from a movie) smiling at you and saying, "You're going to be okay."

Go outside and take a photo of something you find beautiful or interesting.

Breathe in through your nose for a count of 4, hold it for a count of 4, then exhale through your mouth for a count of 8.

Lay on the floor. Squeeze every muscle in your body and hold it for 5 seconds, then relax. Repeat.

Make a phone call to a friend and be honest about the good and the bad in your life. Tell them you don't need advice, just listening.

Allow yourself to opt out of an obligation (like hosting Christmas or celebrating July 4th.)

Go do something that gives you pleasure (a walk, going out for ice cream, saying yes to a kind invitation.)

ACTIVITY

- What are the top 2 worst things people said to you about suicide?
- What are the top 2 best things people said to you?

CERTIFICATE *of* ACHIEVEMENT

1. _____

2. _____

WORST

Wow!

CERTIFICATE *of* ACHIEVEMENT

1. _____

2. _____

BEST

Wow!

My older son helps me decide not to sell the house. We plant lots of flowers instead.

One year later we have a funeral service to bury some of Don's ashes in a beautiful Catholic cemetery. Before I purchase the plot a wonderful woman who works at the church gives me a "tour" of all the people who are buried near Don. She tells me about who they were. Don's new next-door neighbor loved to play cards.

We're all doing the best we can. It's a blur.

3. Becky and her family marked the first anniversary of their loved one's death with a beautiful ceremony at the cemetery. There were several light-hearted moments.

- How have you marked anniversaries? If not, how would you like to?

- Have there been any funny or light-hearted moments in the midst of remembering _____?

- In what ways did _____ try their best?

_____

_____

_____

_____

_____

_____

_____

_____

_____

After three years I'm still getting rid of Don's clutter. I resent it at times and feel very sad at other times.

4. Getting rid of Don's possessions was difficult for Becky.

• When were _____'s possessions dealt with?

• Where did they go?

• If you kept any treasured objects, what were they?

• What feelings did you experience going through "the stuff"?

• Did you stay in the same home or did you leave it?

• What meaning did you find in their belongings?

ACTIVITY

Choose an activity that feels the most healing for you.

Ask a friend to sit with you while you declutter.

Rearrange the furniture in one room. Have fun with it.

Whenever a friend or family member comes over, offer an object for them to keep or give away.

Clean out one drawer today.

_____

_____

_____

_____

_____

5. Becky talks to Don when she visits him in the cemetery.

- Do you still feel connected to _____? If so, how?
- If you're still early in your healing process, can you imagine that at some point you'll feel better?
- What can't you let go of that you cherish?
- What can't you let go of that's keeping you stuck?
- If a significant amount of time has passed, what are the signs of your healing or even thriving?

_____

_____

_____

_____

_____

_____

_____

_____

My husband remains intact in my heart but the pain of his death is no longer a part of my daily life. As I've said, there are many, many things I cherish about Don and our marriage; they are with me as I honestly share the struggles we've gone through since his suicide. At the cemetery today I told him that it's been up to me to raise the kids, clean up the mess his death created and build an entirely new life, which I've succeeded in doing, with many hurdles and rewards along the way. At this point, life is about these accomplishments. It's difficult but I need to claim them as I move into the next phase of my life.

At the 10-year mark I feel that the story of Don's death has in some ways reached its conclusion. Something is over for me; I've been forever changed, but I have also felt for a long time that I would eventually reach this moment of completion. And I'm resolved to experience and even enjoy this feeling, at least until the next thing comes along to resurrect my sense of loss. Each time that happens, though, the pain subsides a little bit sooner.

ACTIVITY

OR

THIS

Visit a place that reminds you of

_____.

Tell them how you're doing, both good and bad. Take a few moments to breathe deeply and listen.

THAT

Choose an activity that

_____

used to enjoy doing. Invite a friend to come along and talk about your memories, both good and bad.

BONUS ACTIVITY

Write, doodle, or draw your answers to the following questions.

What do you wish you had said to _____ before they died?

What do you regret saying to _____ before they died?

If you could somehow get a message to _____ right now, what would you say?

Write a goodbye letter to _____, sharing your thoughts and your feelings.

For Therapists, Educators, and Facilitators

GROUP ACTIVITY 1 WEATHERING FEELINGS

You can use this activity in several ways:

A. Photocopy the weather description cards on the next page and cut them up into a deck. Place them in front of each person in the group for their turn. Read the following statements and after each one ask the person to choose the weather condition card that best describes their feeling.

B. Photocopy a weather description page for each participant. Have them write the question number in each weather area they choose to answer the question. Invite them to talk about their choices.

1. How did you feel right before you found out about the death?
2. How did you feel when you found out?
3. How did you feel right after you found out?
4. How did/do you feel your family members reacted to the death?
5. How did/do you feel about suicide?
6. How did/do you feel telling people about the suicide?
7. How did/do you feel going back to school or work?
8. How did/do you feel seeing relatives?
9. How did/do you feel seeing your parent's or children's reaction to your loss?
10. How did/do you feel about your own many feelings?
11. How did/do you feel about being at home?

42

Foggy	Hurricane
Long Rainstorm	Soft, Warm Breeze
Sandstorm	Partly Cloudy
Cool Mist	Tornado
Avalanche	Wildfire
Sleet	Blizzard
Drought	Hot & Humid
Lightning & Thunder	Warm & Sunny

A Story Portrait is a visual expression of a traumatic experience. Making a Story Portrait using photographic images can offer healing insight. Each Story Portrait is unique to the person creating it. There are no rules and there is no right or wrong way to do it. See examples on the next page.

What you'll need

- Blank printer paper: 3 sheets taped side to side, for each participant
- Tape
- Scissors
- Glue sticks
- Marker(s), black or several colors
- Various magazines with colorful and interesting images

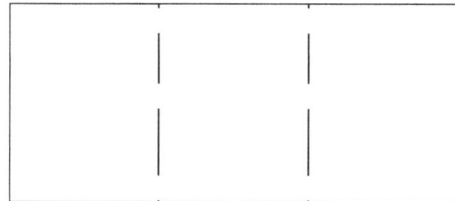

Questions offered as a guideline participants can respond to

Sheet 1. What was going on in your life right before your special person's suicide (or any other loss you'd like to work with)?

Sheet 2. How did you respond to the death or loss? What was a low point for you? What brought you comfort that you were grateful for?

Sheet 3. What have you learned about yourself from this experience? What have you learned about others?

Create the Story Portrait

Tell participants they can respond to all of the questions or maybe only one. Sometimes finding words to express what they're feeling is difficult. Images can be helpful when there are no words.

You may find it helpful to have images cut out in advance, or they can flip through the image sources to cut out and paste as they create their Story Portrait. They might express themselves with words, symbols, and images or just with images.

Sharing

If participants want to share what they created and talk about what the images mean to them, allow time at the end. This can be a very healing experience.

TRAGEDY

I'm stupid

why me?

How do I make this go away?

worthless

I hate it

So much anger

It doesn't make sense

Will it ever be okay?

It could have been me

Shock. Sadness. Guilt. Dark.

So many questions

we are all gifts to each other.

There are so many things to love and live for.

The world is a beautiful place

GROUP ACTIVITY 3 BEFORE AND AFTER

Supplies:

- Sheet of tin foil
- Piece of cardboard
- Sharpies

With a generous sheet of tin foil, ask them to study the foil and recognize how smooth and shiny it is — almost perfect. This is how it can feel prior to the death.

Now read the following statements out loud. If they can relate to the statement you've read, they should make a wrinkle or fold in their foil. They can make a small or a big wrinkle or fold depending on how big they feel the change has been for them.

Change Statements:

"Since the death of my special person..."

1. My friendships have changed.

2. There is less fighting at home.

3. There is more fighting at home.

4. I get angry a lot — even over little things.

5. My home feels really different.

6. I have a lot more questions.

7. I worry more about who else might die.

8. I have a lot of questions about suicide and wonder why they killed themselves.

9. My parent cries a lot more.

10. I want to talk or share less.

11. I can't stop thinking about it.

12. I feel numb — almost like nothing happened.

13. I have more anxiety or fears now.

14. I feel like EVERYTHING has changed.

15. I feel more peaceful.

16. I sometimes feel like I'm to blame for what happened.

17. I feel like my role and responsibilities in the family have changed.

18. It's harder for me to concentrate at school or work.

19. People treat me differently.

20. I am more uncomfortable talking about suicide.

21. I am more comfortable talking about suicide.

22. I won't get this close to anyone else so I won't get hurt again.

23. I want a replacement for the one I lost because I'm afraid to be alone.

The foil may now be in a ball, or have many wrinkles in it. Say, "This ball of foil can feel like your grief right now — all bound up and holding really hard, complicated feelings."

"Now let's carefully smooth your foil out again, and wrap it around this piece of cardboard."

Allow time for them to do this.

"As you look at your foil piece now, it's smooth again but will never be like it was before. The creases, wrinkles, and tears will always be there, just like your grief, but it will get better. It will be smooth again, and feel whole, but you'll never forget and it will never be exactly the same as it was before."

Give them sharpies and ask them to draw something they hope for on their foil.

Helpful Resources

A Guide For Friends: What to Say... and What Not to Say

Reprinted from The Dinner Party and Option B

Many of us experience times when we don't know what to say to a grieving loved one or friend. We worry that we'll say the wrong thing, so we say nothing at all. We tell ourselves people need space when we're really just avoiding our own feelings. We end up repeating the lines of a greeting card verbatim.

The founders of The Dinner Party — an organization that connects mostly 20- and 30-somethings who have experienced significant loss to one another for bi-monthly potluck meals — asked their community about the best and worst things people said to them when they were struggling. Their insights can help you support your friends who have lost a loved one to suicide.

1 Let them know you're thinking of them.

The death of a loved one can feel really isolating. Your friend may feel uncomfortable around people who still have the parent, spouse, child or other loved one they've lost. Or they might not want to let their feelings out around others. But you can help them feel supported while respecting their need for space.

One way to help a grieving friend feel less alone is to simply remind them that you care. Ask how they are doing today. Tell them you're ready for their real answer — fine, terrible, a shrug — without judgment. This lets your friend know they can let their guard down and that you're there for them.

2 Don't wait for someone to tell you how you can help.

"Let me know if there's anything I can do." "Don't hesitate to call if you need anything."

However well-intentioned, these general offers to help rarely work. Few people like asking for assistance, and in the immediate aftermath of loss, people struggle to name what they need.

Instead of offering to "do anything," be as specific as possible about how you can help. Volunteer to create a schedule for friends who want to drop off meals, run out to buy toilet paper, babysit, or mow the lawn. By suggesting something specific, you take the onus off your friend to define what they need.

> "'I can't imagine what you're going through, but I want to help. I'm going shopping tomorrow; do you need anything from the supermarket? This kind of statement didn't try to negate or obscure the emotional reality of the moment but was very focused on a specific question and offered a specific service."
>
> — Esther, Los Angeles

3 Remember that grieving is a process — and it's different for everyone.

Most platitudes are born out of good intentions. We want to lessen the blow, find a silver lining, or fix the unfixable. But reassurances like "Everything happens for a reason" gloss over pain and can deepen the feeling of isolation after loss.

Acknowledge your friend's loss and meet them where they are in the grieving process. Rather than running away from their discomfort, try sitting with it. You don't have to fill every silence. But don't be afraid to ask questions, even if you're afraid of the answer. Just be sure to stick around to hear it.

Resist projecting your own experience onto others. Too often mainstream notions of grief fail to appreciate how people from different backgrounds, cultures, and religions respond to loss. Let your friend be their own best expert on how to move forward.

> "Months after my dad died, I was driving with my high school best friend in silence and suddenly she said, 'So...your dad died. How are you feeling about that?' After weeks of people tiptoeing around the subject and not meeting my eye, it was so incredibly refreshing to have someone confront this fact head-on."
>
> — Hannah, New York

4 Don't be afraid to talk about the people your friends have lost.

It's important to make space to remember the people we've lost. The late best-selling author and health care reform advocate Elizabeth Edwards once gave an interview in which she talked about how friends hesitated to bring up her son who had died. They didn't want to remind her of one of the most painful chapters in her life. The truth was, she hadn't forgotten about that chapter. She never would. And she loved knowing that others remembered her son fondly too.

Ask questions about the people your friends have lost. Try openers like "Tell me about your mom..." or "I wish I'd had the chance to meet your friend Tim. What's one of your favorite stories about him?"

Don't try to force these conversations, and always follow your friend's lead. But remember that not every memory is sad, and conversations about those we've lost don't have to be either.

> "I really appreciate it when people ask about my dad's life and not just about his death."
>
> — Anonymous Dinner Party Attendee

5 Show up for your friends immediately after their loss.

Losing someone we love is deeply unmooring. Suddenly, the world feels different. We look for reassurances that we haven't lost everything we had the day before.

Show your grieving friends that you're still there for them. Offer to treat them to a movie or go on a hike — an activity that you would have done in the past but that doesn't require a lot of conversation. Some people choose to keep themselves busy after loss. Don't try to stop them. Instead, ask how you can help. Above all, follow their cues.

6 Stick around past the initial wave of support.

When it comes to grief, the initial period of intense mourning only tells part of the story. The way people experience grief changes over time, but there's no such thing as going back, moving on, or getting over it. Years later, people may no longer identify as grieving, but they remain no less affected by the experience of losing someone they love.

Your friends will need your ongoing support as they navigate their loss. Make sure to continue small acts of kindness to remind them that you're still thinking of them as the surge of initial attention after loss fades.

> "Eight years after my mom passed, in the midst of exciting professional opportunities, the grief finally caught up with me and I decided I needed to take a sabbatical... What helped me most during that time was everyone's unconditional understanding and support."
>
> — Christina, San Francisco

For more information, visit thedinnerparty.org and optionb.org.

Safe Messaging

The way we talk about suicide can raise general awareness that suicide is a serious public health problem that can be prevented. We can help reduce the stigma so that people who need help feel safe enough to ask for it.

When you're talking to people in the community or on social media:

- Don't glorify or romanticize suicide or people who have died by suicide.
- Don't normalize suicide by presenting it as a common event.
- Don't present suicide as an inexplicable act.
- Don't explain suicide only as a result of stress.
- Don't focus on personal details of people who have died by suicide.
- Don't give overly detailed descriptions of suicide methods.

- Do emphasize help-seeking and provide information on finding help (see Helpful Resources below).
- Do emphasize prevention.
- Do list warning signs of suicide.
- Do highlight treatment for underlying mental health problems.

Helpful Organizations

If you or someone else is at immediate risk of suicide, call 911.

National Suicide Prevention Lifeline: 1-800-273-8255

Crisis Text Line: text 741741

Trevor Project (LGBTQ): 1-866-488-7386 / thetrevorproject.org

Trans Lifeline: hotline 877-565-8860 / translifeline.org

American Foundation for Suicide Prevention: afsp.org

National Alliance on Mental Illness (NAMI): nami.org

NAMI Minnesota: 1-888-626-4435 / namimn.org

Warning Signs of Suicide

Warning signs are behaviors that family, friends, or acquaintances may notice about people who are thinking about suicide. If you observe these behaviors, please don't ignore them. People who display these warning signs should be asked directly if they are thinking of killing themselves. If the answer is yes, they should be referred to a qualified professional for a risk assessment.

- Threatening to hurt or kill themselves or talking about wanting to hurt or kill themselves.
- Seeking access to firearms, pills, or other means to kill themselves.
- Talking or writing about death, dying, or suicide.
- Acting recklessly or engaging in risky activities without considering the consequences.
- Increasing alcohol or drug use.
- Seeming anxious or agitated, being unable to sleep, or sleeping a lot.
- Appearing hopeless.
- Showing rage, uncontrolled anger, or seeking revenge.
- Seeming trapped, like there's no way out.
- Withdrawing from friends, family, and wider community.
- Showing dramatic mood changes.
- Seeming to have no reason for living and no sense of purpose in life.

Direct Verbal Cues:
- "I wish I was dead."
- "I'm going to end it all."
- "If such and such doesn't happen, I'll kill myself."

Less Direct Verbal Cues:
- "You'll be better off without me."
- "I'm so tired of it all."
- "What's the point of living?"
- "Who cares if I'm dead anyway?"

If you feel someone is in immediate danger, call 911 or an ambulance to take them to the emergency room. Do not leave the person unattended, even briefly.

988 Suicide & Crisis Lifeline

Call or text 988 if you or a loved one is experiencing a mental health crisis.

The 988 Suicide & Crisis Lifeline can be reached by calling or texting 988 or chating 988lifeline.org for themselves or if they are worried about a loved one who may need crisis support.

988 serves as a universal entry point so that no matter where you live in the United States, you can reach a trained crisis counselor who can help.

988 offers 24/7 access to trained crisis counselors who provide free and confidential emotional support to help people experiencing mental health-related distress. That could be:

- Thoughts of suicide
- Mental health or substance use crisis, or
- Any other kind of emotion distress

REBECCA ANDERSON, LPN, LCSW, mother, medical professional, educator, and speaker, with a BS in Public Health/Sociology, is the author of *Parenting the Suicide Survivors' Club* and co-founder of SSC, LLC. She's worked as a nurse in maternal/child healthcare and as a medical social worker. Rebecca lost her husband to suicide in 2002. Eight years later she and her children embarked on a healing art/narrative journey with artist Laurie Phillips that resulted in the *Suicide Survivors' Club* 5-book set. She co-presents *Trauma Transformed Through Art and Narrative.*

LAURIE PHILLIPS, artist, healer, author, speaker, and co-founder of SSC, LLC has worked as a public artist since 1992. She's served as a stress relief coach in hospitals and other organizations and is the co-founder of Museum Sage, an experience that combines life coaching and art appreciation. Laurie and Rebecca have co-presented on using art and narrative to heal from a traumatic experience at Mayo Clinic, NAMI Minnesota, American Association of Suicidology, Macalester College, and Children's Hospital.

www.ingramcontent.com/pod-product-compliance
Lightning Source LLC
Chambersburg PA
CBHW041426090426
42741CB00002B/57